Be still ~ move on in peace

Barbara Ellen

authorHOUSE®

AuthorHouse™ UK Ltd.
500 Avebury Boulevard
Central Milton Keynes, MK9 2BE
www.authorhouse.co.uk
Phone: 08001974150

First published by AuthorHouse 1/25/2010

ISBN: 978-1-4490-6956-8 (sc)

This book is printed on acid-free paper.

This book is dedicated to all my loved ones.

I always thought that I was special.

I was very much loved by my parents. I felt it every day and their unconditional love and admiration of me has walked beside me in what has been such a happy life. I think now that they laid the groundwork for what was to come.

I have a secret.

I first noticed laughter in a river.

I was walking early to work along the concrete path beside a river in the middle of a city. The sun was shimmering on a wide swathe of still water. The shimmering changed to individual spots of light that glittered, danced and laughed with me when I smiled.

My arms tingled, starting with my fingertips. My head filled with happiness and my throat choked with tears.

I looked forward to it every morning after that. After a while it seemed quite normal, but so exciting at the same time.

Not a good idea to tell anyone. I was a grown up lady, for goodness sake! It happened every day, even without sunshine. The sparkling and laughter walked with me until I reluctantly had to turn towards my office.

Not long after, I was sitting on a park bench in my lunch hour munching through my sandwiches. It was Autumn, a still day, and golden leaves crunched under my feet.

I noticed nearby a big blackbird watching me. We studied each other for a while. Suddenly there was a flurry of wind in front of my knees. It picked up dozens of leaves and whirled them round and round, higher and higher. The air turned a brilliant blue and shimmered all around me for many minutes and I heard laughter. My fingertips tingled. The sensation moved up my arms and over my whole body. Again, I was moved to tears. The blackbird flew away.

This was twenty years ago, and, whatever or whoever had finally managed to show itself to me, is with me all the time.

We now live our lives together on a daily, even hourly basis.

Barbara Ellen

About twelve years ago, I'd reached a point in my life where I'd changed all the things that weren't right for me anymore. I knew who I wanted to be with and what sort of life I wanted to live.
Unfortunately patience doesn't come easily to a sagittariun woman!

Sitting in a different office in a different job, I started writing...disjointed sentences, odd words, but all so full of hope and comfort. Sometimes my writings were days apart, sometimes weeks. I kept them all.

Then I started drawing too. Wonderful spheres of shimmering light. Always six of them. My own image walking towards encircling arms. I started dating everything and tucking them into a file.

My 'journal' was born.

13th September 1996

Wait ~ patience ~ make no noise ~ we will help you ~ leave things to us ~ we are always with you.
Now only do you begin to hear us.

16th September 1996

Wait ~ you will see what you've been waiting for ~ we will take away your fears ~ better than you'd even hoped for ~ as planned ~ we are with you ~ we won't go away.
Be still.

25th September 1996

It's part of the plan ~ take heart ~ changes are happening all the time ~ be strong ~ you're learning patience, but you falter ~ you'll be together when the leaves turn and are thick on the ground ~ we're with you always.
Be still.

25th September 1996

Comfort ~ Friend ~ Companion ~ Trust ~ Mentor ~ Teacher.

30th September 1996

Gentle ~ soft ~ wonderful ~ autumn ~ happiness ~ together.

5th October 1996

You can wait ~ you still have more to learn ~ life is waiting for you ~ let it evolve ~ we are here ~ there's much happiness to come.

10th November 1996

Waiting ~ thinking ~ autumn ~ garden ~ leaves ~ corner ~ seat ~ wind ~ comfort ~ togetherness ~ gentle ~ laughter ~ woodsmoke ~ future.
Don't leave us.

Barbara Ellen

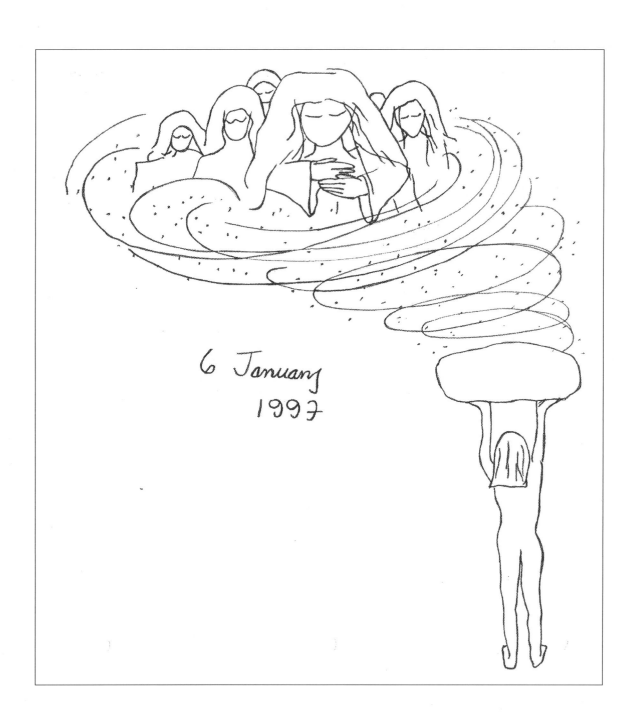

6 January
1997

Be Still ~ Move On In Peace

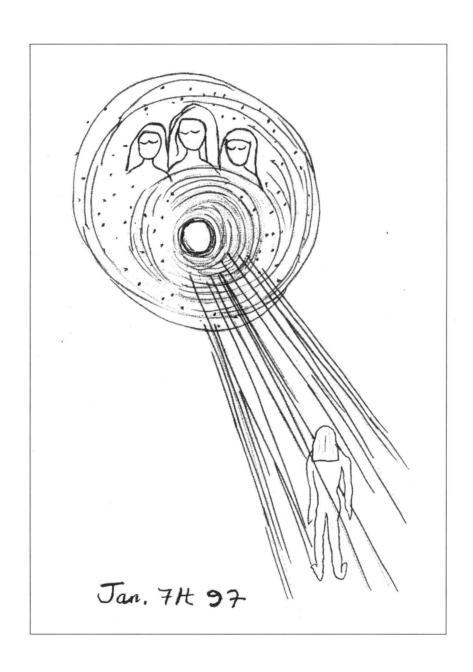

Jan. 7th 97

January 12 '97

Be Still ~ Move On In Peace

Be Still ~ Move On In Peace

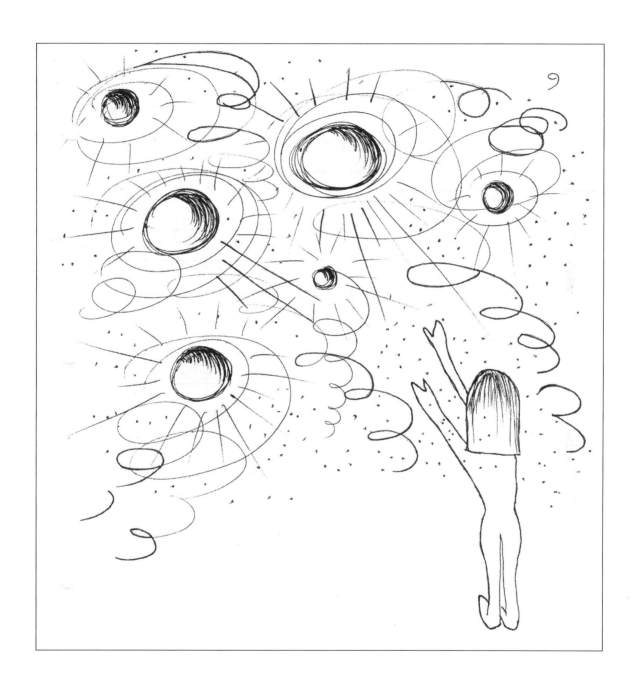

Barbara Ellen

19TH February 97

Be Still ~ Move On In Peace

Barbara Ellen

21ST February 97

Be Still ~ Move On In Peace

24 February '97

Barbara Ellen

16th April '97

Be Still ~ Move On In Peace

24 April 97

27TH May 97

Be Still ~ Move On In Peace

11th June 1997

It's all in the great order of things ~ you're on the right path ~ follow whatever life brings ~it's meant to be ~ great happiness awaits. It's near.

17

8th July '97

18

25ᵗʰ July 97

19

26 August '97

Be Still ~ Move On In Peace

27th August 1997

You have to believe in us ~ we have shown you all that can happen ~ and has ~ great happiness is there ~ it's the next thing to happen ~ press forward and be with us.

You have stepped into the light.

2nd September 97

Be Still ~ Move On In Peace

He has his back to you ~ you are walking up behind him ~ soon he will turn around and you will know.
You have no reason to be nervous ~ we are here for you.
Take heart.

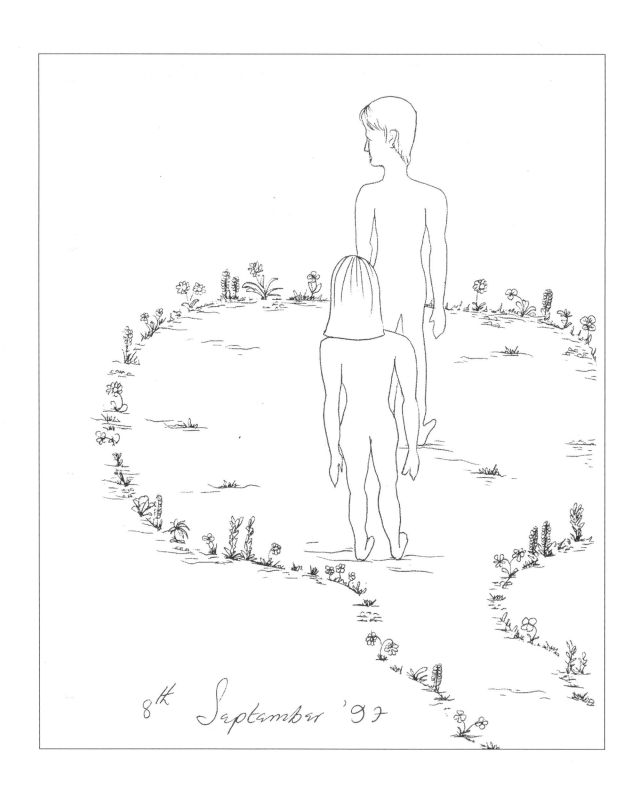

8th September '97

Be Still ~ Move On In Peace

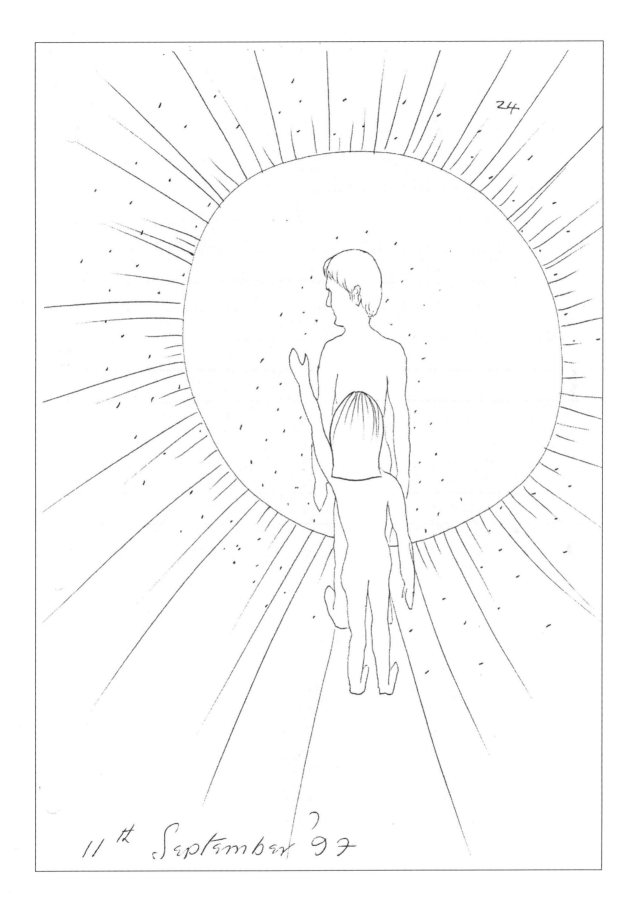

11th September '97

16th September 1997

When all is peaceful and soft winds are sweeping the grass, you will remember our words and all that we promised.

You will then be fulfilled.

Be not afraid to give of yourself fully. He will not let you down.

In the leaves you will hear us ~ golden, dancing and thick on the ground.

Just wait.   All you desire will become yours.

19th September 1997

Look to yourself ~ we are with you and working for you ~ be not afraid ~ have no doubts ~ all is near ~ so wonderful.

You have the freedom to be happy.

Take heart.

7th October 1997

He is waiting ~ you need do nothing ~ be open to receive him ~ he will not pass you by.

Be patient.

All will be yours.

He has seen you, but does not know yet.

15th October 1997

He is there.

He is looking at you.

Do not be afraid.

It's time.

Your path has been leading to this.

17th October 1997

Your path is set.

You have travelled far.

Take what we can give and enjoy it.

There is much happiness to come.

21st October 1997

We will bring him to you.

He is here.

Do not imagine what we have planned for you ~ only we know.

It will not be long.

Enjoy your home a little longer ~ soon you will create a new life with a long term partner.

He will want it and so will you.

Stay with us.

23ʳᵈ October 1997

When you walk into the light, you walk with us.

We are your friends.

We are with you always.

Never doubt the faith we have in you.

You have the ability to succeed in whatever you do.

Take life and enjoy it.

Follow your instincts.

We're here.

24th October 1997

Be at peace with us.

Be at peace with yourself.

We will fulfil you.

Only now do you become to know us and all we can do.

 Doubt not our power.

Be still.

4th November 1997

You can have him if you want him.

You are changing.

You have brought him to you.

We are proud of you.

13th November 1997

Open your mind.

All is well.

The leaves will be thicker and the path will be set.

2nd December 1997

We are here.

You left us for a while of your own free will.

You need not doubt us.

Be strong ~ do not succumb to doubts and fears.

If you only knew what happiness awaits.

23rd December 1997

Listen to the words of your friends ~ they have a message for you.

Your patience is not your strength. No matter ~ we have enough patience for you ~ all is close ~ you cannot imagine what.

Our power is infinite.

21st January 1998

Be us with always.

We are here for you.

Our time is different from your time.

You are learning all the time.

Just wait ~ each day you become stronger ~ each day is important.

You know us more and what we can do.

We feel your faith in us ~ now it is more accepting.

When you completely trust us, all will be yours.

11th February 1998

We are with you ~ taking care of you ~ you are learning more about us ~ your life has become more serene ~ now it is time to move on to the next part.

Great happiness awaits.

You know that happiness must come from the soul and not from others.

You are now ready to meet your love.

Be ready.

12TH February '98

Be Still ~ Move On In Peace

16th March 1998

You are learning more about us ~ you have to believe in us ~ we have shown you what we can do together ~ none of your dreams are impossible ~ travel with us ~ we will not forsake you.

Wondrous things are in store.

20th April 1998

Give us your love and we will give you the world.

1st May 1998

Stay with us ~ be with us ~ do not waver ~ all is nearly complete ~ are you ready.

Your heart will open like a flower and the dew will nurture it ~ such love is still to come ~ a love that will last a lifetime and endure all hardships.

6th May '98

Be Still ~ Move On In Peace

19th May 1998

Come with us ~ be with us.

Some people you cannot help and will have to leave behind.

We will take you on a journey to a magical new land.

You will be safe and all will be well.

Be not afraid of change.

You will find great happiness.

28th May 1998

If all does not seem to happen at once, take heart ~ the slower will be the stronger.

There will be much confusion in your new love's heart ~ he will know the way to go however.

Such happiness awaits.

15th June 1998

He will be with you soon ~ you have waited so long.

We have always been with you.

Get to know him a little longer.

He has always been journeying towards you.

Enjoy this beginning.

16th June 1998

This is fun, isn't it ?

18th June 1998

Ending will be hard, but not as hard as you think.

You have time still to decide, but to leave is inevitable.

You cannot look behind you.

All your happiness lies before you.

2nd July 1998

You will be happy ~ he will want you ~ you only have to be yourself.

Take time to enjoy the next part ~ be ready for your new beginning.

We will take care of you.

Be strong.

21st July 1998

Should you falter, we will help you.

Should you stumble, we will pick you up.

You have given yourself over to our hands.

We will not fail you.

Some people search for a lifetime for the contentment you feel now ~ we feel it too.

 Your joy is our joy.

Be still.

5th August 1998

You are with us.

Be with us.

All we promised shall come true ~ you feel the stirring of a new life ~ it soon will be yours.

You have shown much patience.

Share these things with others.

20th August 1998

He will be will you when the time is ready.

Do not doubt us ~ we are here for you.

When the time is right it will not fail.

You have learnt that two doves cannot dwell together before their time.

Stay with us and we will show you great happiness.

20th August '98

28th August 1998

Wait for us ~ we are your friends ~ all is not as you perceive ~ great happiness awaits ~ we know you have faith in us.

 We are moving things towards you ~ the slower will be the stronger ~ he is already with you.

2nd September 1998

There is much in life you don't understand.

We have a wider view of things ~ some events need to happen first before your life can evolve.

You know it will happen ~ you can feel it.

You have already walked in the garden, through the mist around the trees and through the wet grass.

You can already feel his love.

Just wait a little longer.

You know him.

Be with us.

3rd September 1998

We are with you.

When you sense someone behind you, it is us.

You wished to see us ~ soon you will.

Until then know that we are with you always.

Listen to the words of your friends.

10th September 1998

Would you want things to happen that you know wouldn't be right ~ just to curb your impatience.

We are taking care of you and your future life.

Take heart.

23rd September 1998

Take our words and listen.

You know now our time span is not yours.

Enjoy this time.

Take heart.

Be Still ~ Move On In Peace

July 1982

12th November '98

He will be with you soon ~ it will come by surprise.

You're happy, aren't you.

We're happy.

Ending one part of your life wasn't as hard as you thought it would be.

Be strong.

We're always with you.

9th December 1998

Do you feel it?

It's coming nearer~ when you least expect it.

Do you want him? Then you can have him.

All will be revealed soon.

Only you can feel us, hear us ~ at the moment.

18th December 1998

You will see us soon.

You will not be afraid.

Trust your new awareness and use it carefully.

We will give you extra gifts to help people.

Follow your instincts.

21st December 1998

We are with you.

Can you feel us?

Can you feel him? He is in your heart already and you are in his.

This time ahead will be well spent.

Take care. Take heart.

We will never leave you.

14th January 1999

See us in the sky ~ feel our delight.

Your world is now our world ~ soon you will see us.

Don't despair anymore ~ just wait for the right time.

Enjoy this ending and look to your new beginning.

14th Januari 1999

1st February 1999

Don't be afraid ~ it's the next step.

All this was meant to happen.

Look ahead ~ see your new man and your new life.

We are with always.

18th February 1999

All things are happening to you now.

Did you believe us?

We will show you the way to go and take care of you.

Do not doubt us.

This is the start of something new.

Do not look back.

26th May 1999

There is still more learning for you.

We are still paving your way.

All will be well ~ we are taking care of everything.

Your dreams will be fulfilled soon.

Take heart.

Do not leave us.

18 th June '99

Welcome Home Princess

Love

John

xxx

18th June 1999

8th July 1999

Did we not tell you great happiness awaited.

We will take care of everything.

Your daughter will be fine ~ she too will find a new man and know great happiness.

July 26th 1999

We told you what you needed to do ~ and to be.

We will still help you with your doubts.

We are glad you are happy.

It was your time.

We are always here.

26th July '89

16th August 1999

We will lead you.

We will lead others too.

Do not falter.

Your path is set.

There is still much happiness to come.

We accept your thanks and are glad that you are happy.

24th August '99

27th August 1999

We will show you the way.

You have taken the first step.

Nothing is too small for us.

You have earned this and will do well.

We will help you and be with you always.

We will always take care of you.

13th September 1999

We are here for you always ~ you do not need to ask for anything ~ we know what you need.

We will take care of your children and loved ones too.

Be with us.

Daddy says Hello.

7th June 2000

Seraphina { Serah}

Veronicah { Verah}

Magdalena

13th June 2000

Francesca

Riah

Nonah

14th August 2001

If we give you this gift, will you give this gift away to inspire others?

There is too much doubt in the world.

Hope is so powerful.

It needs only one ray against clouds of doubt.

Anything can be achieved if you trust in us.

We will care for you and you loved ones.

You can always come to us for help for others.

Be happy, be strong and trust in us to do the best for you

 and everyone else in your life.

27th July 2001

I thank you, my angels, for my life so unbearably sweet ~ a good man who loves me and protects me in all ways.

My son of whom I'm so proud ~ he made his own way ~ he has reason to be proud of himself.

My daughters ~ so strong ~ so funny ~ so lovable ~ cleverer and brighter than me ~ goodness! There's a thing!

However long you give me this gift, I thank you for my destiny and happiness.

I know I falter along the way, but thank you.

Barbara Ellen.